Keys to the Maze

Poems for Purposeful Living
By Wayne Visser

I0161509

Paperback edition published in 2024

by Kaleidoscope Futures, Narborough, UK.

Cover photography and design by Wayne Visser.

Printing and distribution by Lulu.com.

978-1-908875-96-9

Non-fiction Books by Wayne Visser

Beyond Reasonable Greed

South Africa: Reasons to Believe

Corporate Citizenship in Africa

Business Frontiers

The A to Z of Corporate Social
    Responsibility

Making A Difference

Landmarks for Sustainability

The Top 50 Sustainability Books

The World Guide to CSR

The Age of Responsibility

The Quest for Sustainable Business

Corporate Sustainability & Responsibility

CSR 2.0

Disrupting the Future

This is Tomorrow

Sustainable Frontiers

The CSR International Research
    Compendium: Volumes 1-3

The World Guide to Sustainable Enterprise:
    Volumes 1-4

The Little Book of Quotations on Social
    Responsibility

The Little Book of Quotations on
    Sustainable Business

The Little Book of Quotations on
    Transformational Change

Purpose Inspired: Reflections on Conscious
    Living: Volumes 1-5

Thriving: The Breakthrough Movement to
    Regenerate Nature, Society and the
    Economy

Everyday Inspiration: Philosophy for Daily
    Living

Fiction Books by Wayne Visser

I Am An African: Favourite Africa Poems

Wishing Leaves: Favourite Nature Poems

Seize the Day: Favourite Inspirational
    Poems

String, Donuts, Bubbles and Me: Favourite
    Philosophical Poems

African Dream: Inspiring Words & Images
    from the Luminous Continent

Icarus: Favourite Love Poems

About the Author

Dr Wayne Visser is a globally recognised "pracademic", poet and "possibilist". Chat GPT 4o lists him as one of the world's top 10 academics in regenerative business, innovation and technology. He has faculty roles at the University of Cambridge and Católica Porto Business School. He is also director of the thinktank Kaleidoscope Futures, founder of CSR International, and former director of Sustainability Services at KPMG and strategy analyst at Capgemini. He has written 45 books, including eight previous collections of poetry, five Purpose Inspired volumes, and two works of fiction. He has travelled to 83 countries, and lives with his wife, Indira, in Norfolk, UK.

Website: www.waynevisser.com

Email: wayne@waynevisser.com

Contents

Keys to the Maze

Upon the path of life's great maze
Surprises lurk around each bend
There may be dragons, spells or gold
And battles fought before the end

And on this journey to the heart
Of life's great mysteries
You'll have to unlock secret doors
That need some special keys

The first key is IDENTITY –
The quest to know your mind
It helps you bypass cul-de-sacs
And treasure what you find

The second key is CONFIDENCE –
The will to stretch and strive
It takes you where you want to go
And keeps your hopes alive

The third's RESPONSIBILITY –
Your footprint on the earth
It means you care for where you tread
And know what life is worth

The fourth key is the shape of LOVE –
With enigmatic flame of red
It burns the heart; it warms the cold
And lights the way ahead

The fifth key is life's MEANING –
The pattern in the maze
It finds a way to join the dots
With destiny's bright blaze

I wish you happy twists and turns
On easy trails and steep
Whatever choices that you make
These keys are yours to keep.

Waves and Cranes

The waves lick and lap, froth and churn
Rising and crashing, every way we turn
The waves are endless, relentless
Rippling when calm, frightening in a
    tempest
What can we do but learn the tide
Build a strong boat and strap in for the ride

The cranes strut and flap, preen and soar
Rising and gliding, from mountain to shore
The cranes are timeless, full of grace
Stretched out in flight, they're masters of
    space
What can we do but learn the sky
Grow our own wings and do our best to fly.

Into the Deep

It's dusky dark down here, and it's colder
Below the blinding surface light of day
It's endless here and timeless, it's older
Beneath the frothing churn and swirling
    fray
This is where I marvel at waxing words
That grow like corals on a rugged reef
Here my winged thoughts can swoop like
    bright birds
And soar on currents swooning blue and
    deep

It's stretched down here and open, it's
    tranquil
Unlike the noisy clang of cluttered lands
It's serenely slow here, and it's thankful
Not like the stormy seas of grabbing hands
This is where I revel in siren songs
That dart like silver fish, that sway and
    sweep
Here my spirit searches, it lurks and longs
To plumb the murky mysteries of the deep

It's safe down here and secure, it's calming
Beyond the clamouring and cloying crowds
It's sacred ground here, and it's embalming
Laying the past to rest in healing shrouds
This is where my shapeshifting shadow
        rears
Up like a mythic kraken from its sleep
Here my psyche faces its furtive fears
And swims with silent sharks that stalk the
        deep

It's curiously quiet here, and stranger
Than ordered life on the surface above
It's different here, and not without danger
Yet all the risks are in service of love
This is where I worship the gods of art
And witness sculptures dance and
        paintings speak
Here my love affairs bud from eye to heart
As sultry seduction stirs in the deep

It's much wilder down here, it's more
    freeing
For the mind can explore farther reaches
It's more creative here, there's more
    dreaming
And I hear what inspiration teaches
This simulacrum of birth and death
Is an incubator where insights leap
Where I learn to value my every breath
Each time I dive to the infinite deep.

Scroll On

If you're screen scrolling for a fix
Or a daily dose of doom, scroll on
If you're meme surfing for your kicks
Or spoiling for a fight, troll on

Go frolic to your heart's content
In frothing waves that lap and leap
And only when you're fully spent
Dive down with me into the deep.

Unwaveringly Uncertain

In a world that craves certainty
Be unwaveringly uncertain
For nothing is so dangerous
As a person who is certain
Of their own rightness
The world is constantly changing
And uncertainty is the pathway
To knowledge and wisdom

In a world that revels in cacophony
Be resolutely silent
For nothing is so self-defeating
As someone who shouts louder
To be heard above the noise
The world is endlessly babbling
And silence is the secret
To saying more with less

In a world that vies for attention
Be steadfastly focused
For nothing is so futile
As a person who craves affirmation
From fickle strangers
The world is doggedly distracting
And focus is the superpower
For creating real impact

In a world that sows division
Be consciously connected
For nothing is so destructive
As someone who plants seeds of discontent
In fields of insecurity
The world is dazzlingly diverse
And connecting is the fine art
Of leading with love

In a world that favours action
Be deeply reflective
For nothing is so counterproductive
As a person who acts impulsively
Without weighing consequences
The world is forever shifting
And reflection is the discipline
Of studying emerging patterns

In a world that wants simple answers
Be conspicuously complex
For nothing is so misleading
As someone who promises quick fixes
To life's hard problems
The world is strangely entangled
And complexity is the cipher
To decode life's meaning.

Take Me To Your Leader

Take me to your leader –
No, not him, for he acts on a whim
Not him, for he cares not for you
Or me, do you not see?
He cares only for himself:
His plans and his power
His fans and his tower
Is he really your pick?
Take me to your leader –
But not him, surely not him

Take me to your leader –
No, not her, for she's known to defer
Not her, for she speaks not for me
Or you, is it not true?
She speaks only for herself:
Her pawns and her pleasure
Her scorns and her treasure
Is she really your choice?
Take me to your leader –
But not her, surely not her

Take me to your leaders –
No, not them, for they will never bend
Not them, for they act not
On our behalf, are you having a laugh?
They act only for themselves:
Their game and their betting
Their fame and their getting
Are they really who you choose?
Take me to your leaders –
But not them, surely, not them

Take me to your leader –
Yes, she who cares and he who dares
Yes, she who serves and he who deserves
Our loyal pact, is that not a fact?
For they are wise who help others rise:
With hands used for lifting
Through sands ever shifting
Will you rise with the tide?
Take me to your leader –
Yes them, surely them

Take me to your leader –
Ah yes, now I see, who else could it be?
I see now, the leader is you
For you are one of us
Who cares for us and understands:
Our fears and our flying
Our tears and our trying
Ah yes, you have my support
Take me, as our leader –
And I will gladly follow.

Book of Magic

When we are young, we dream of magical
      worlds

Of fairies and wizards making mischief and
      casting spells

Then we grow older, and the story of life
      unfurls

And we give up on the promise of witches
      and wishing wells

For we discover that ordinary life tells a
      different tale

Of incredible feats and secrets hidden in
      plain sight

We discover that magic is alive and the
      quest for the grail

Is about fighting our own dragons and
      pursuing the light

Every day, we hold the Book of Magic in our
hands

Our thoughts and words are powerful spells
we cast

Every year, we discover fantastical new
lands

And learn to see deeper and make the
magic last.

Footnotes

The things we do, the things we say
The hoops we shoot, the games we play
Are beats and riffs within our song
In search of places we belong

The views and detours on the way
Are uncut gems we find in clay
Some stones we polish 'til they shine
The rest we toss and leave behind

No matter what we build and burn
It's how we love and what we learn
That writes the story of our days
The rest are footnotes on the page.

Better With You

My life's been full of ups and downs
With twists and turns to make it through
I could have done it on my own
But frankly, it's better with you

Along the way, I've learned and grown
With tips and tricks to keep it new
I could have made it by myself
But I know, I'm better with you

The way ahead is never straight
With fears and hopes to keep it true
I could have played it solitaire
But always, life's better with you.

Call of the Wild

I hear the howl of the wolf
Mourning
From the shadows of the dying forest
Listen:
Do you hear the wolves howling?

I hear the song of the whale
Beseeching
From the depths of the warming ocean
Hush now:
Do you hear the whales singing?

I hear the cry of the eagle
Pleading
From the heights of the smoking sky
Listen:
Do you hear the eagles crying?

I hear the trumpet of the elephant
Warning
From the swathe of the burning grassland
Quiet now:
Do you hear the elephants trumpeting?

I hear the snort of the buffalo
Deriding
From the breadth of the flooding plain
Listen:
Do you hear the buffaloes snorting?

I hear the saw of the jaguar
Echoing
From the crags of the eroding mountain
Be still:
Do you hear the jaguars sawing?

I hear cough of the kangaroo
Pleading
From the flats of the scorching outback
Listen:
Do you hear the kangaroos coughing?

I hear the honk of the geese
Berating
From the pools of the shrinking wetland
Take note:
Do you hear the geese honking?

I hear the growl of the bear
Cursing
From the floes of the melting iceberg
Listen:
Do you hear the bears growling?

I hear the squeak of the dolphin
Grieving
From the tides of the choking shore
Breathe in:
Do you hear the dolphins squeaking?

I hear the chatter of the ape
Questioning
From the treetops of the receding jungle
Listen:
Do you hear apes chattering?

This is the call of the wild

Inviting us

To take heed and act before it's too late

Even now:

Do you hear the wild calling?

Fairytales

The strange thing about fairytales
Is that they're mostly true
Their meaning hides behind the veils
And therein lies the clue

Each hero's fate, each witch's spell
Each dragon fought and slayed
Reflect within our wishing well
As dreams that flare and fade

For life is full of holy grails
And monsters we must fight
We each must walk enchanted trails
Through darkness to the light

The secret lies not in the quests
Or if we thrive or fail
The wonder's that we face the tests
And live to tell the tale.

An Iridescent Call

A lilting lyric whispers a shadow of darker
    days
An unlucky roll of the loaded dice of chance
A meandering melody rises and falls,
    pitches and sways
A flight on the wing, an open invitation to
    dance

The rhythm is beating, I'm tapping my feet
The singer is singing, I'm feeling the heat
The word clouds are poems, my skies are
    ablaze
The music is swirling, I'm running the maze

A percussive pulse taps a dulcet drum in
    my head
A wave of joy rises like an ocean swell in my
    heart
A vaulting voice flows freely, swirling blue
    and red
A wail of black endings, an iridescent call to
    start.

The Soundtrack of Our Lives

All it takes is a song, a riff, or a note
And I'm transported back, spirited away
I'm a time traveller to somewhere remote
Yet familiar, a place where I used to play

Music is a form of magic, an enchantment
That reveals clues to secrets of the heart
Music is a kind of mushroom, an
    hallucinogen
That opens doors to wild worlds we can
    chart

All it takes is a beat, a hook, or a voice
And we're reconnected, spellbound in a
    blink
We're in the memory maze of fate and
    choice
Reliving our dreams, and dancing in sync.

Rewilding

Our living world may be under threat
But we're not giving up, no not just yet
For we get to say how this tale ends
And it's never too late to make amends

Let's get to know what nature's knowing
And start to sow what nature's sowing
Let's feel the flow of nature's flowing
And start to go where nature's going

Bring back the hunters and the grazers
To recreate life's moods and mazes
Bring back the diggers and dam-makers
To be the shifters and the shapers

For rewilding's about letting go and letting
    be
It's about getting slow and setting free
Rewilding's about thinking big and starting
    small
It's about linking up and standing tall

So let's rewild our rivers, our wetlands and
　　　seas
Our forests and grasslands, our meadows
　　　for bees
Let's rewild our cities, our gardens and
　　　streets
Our factories and farms, where earth and
　　　sky meets

Bring back wild horses, wild boars and wild
　　　bears
The wolves and the badgers that live in
　　　their lairs
Bring back the wild elephants and wild
　　　otters shy
The cheetahs and pumas and eagles that
　　　fly

For rewilding's about taking less and giving
　　　more
It's about making space from mountain to
　　　shore
Rewilding's about seeing beauty in the
　　　tangled mess
It's about trusting more and controlling less

So let's rewild our oceans, our lakes and
      our lands

Our corals and coastlines, our vast desert
      sands

Let's rewild our mindscapes, to be truly
      alive

And give life on this planet its moment to
      thrive

For our living world at last has a chance

To regenerate its bounty in a sacred dance

As we join with nature, moving in sync

We'll rewild the Earth, back from the brink.

If You Believe

Do you believe that the world can be better?

That what comes next is not determined by
what came before

That every choice we make creates a new
nexus of possibility

And every action we take shapes a new
pathway of history?

Do you believe that the future will be
brighter?

That every problem has a solution that can
take us forward

That every setback contains a lesson that
makes us stronger

And every fear hides a dream that was
conceived in love?

Do you believe that the earth can recover?

That the damage we've done does not
preclude nature from healing

That every degraded field is an opportunity
to rewild the land

And every polluted water body is an
invitation to bring back life?

Do you believe that peace can return?

That acts of violence are a vicious cycle that
can be broken

That every conflict is a maze of pain with a
way out

And every aggression is a futile fight with
our own shadow?

Do you believe that all people can thrive?

That yesterday's deprivation does not
prevent tomorrow's fulfilment

That every injustice is a clarion call to take
a stand

And every unmet need is fertile ground to
seed innovation?

Do you believe that our children will
proper?

That their beautiful lives are not shackled
by our legacy of mistakes

That every challenge is a classroom to apply
new learning

And every lifetime is a playground for fresh
imagination?

Because if you believe, then a brighter
 future will dawn

If you believe, then the earth will recover
 and peace will return

If you believe, then people will thrive and
 our children will prosper

If you believe, then nothing – absolutely
 nothing – is impossible

If you believe, you will act to remake our
 world and reshape our future

If you believe, you will care enough to listen
 to the voices of change

If you believe, you will join together to
 harness the power of hope

But first you must believe, for all life begins
 as an audacious act of faith.

The Book of Changes

Part 1.

This is the time of transition
The rhyme of revision
On the cusp
Between dying and being reborn
The dawn of new light
The fight of contraction and deep breathing
Of conviction and deep grieving
On the cusp
Between pain and promise
The rhyme of rain and conflagration
This is the time of expectation

This is the moment of madness
The low point of sadness
On the fringe
Between chaos and new order
The border of old crumbling ways
The maze of fear and deep division
Of hollow cheer and deep schism
On the fringe
Between lies and false prophets
The low point of political scoring
This is the moment of tribes warring

This is the song of soul searching
The long night of mind lurching
On the frontier
Between dogma and new paradigms
The bell chimes of dire warning
The yawning questions of deep reflection
Of poignant lessons for deep inflection
On the frontier
Between scouting and getting lost
The long night of struggling to cope
This is the song of faith and hope

Part 2.

This is the chasm of creation
The spasm of revelation
On the margin
Between black space and star-bursts
The universe like petals unfolding
The moulding of myths and deep reality
Of rippling riffs of deep gravity
On the margin
Between the void and seminal sparks
The spasm of pregnant desires
This is the chasm of forging fires

This is the time of transformation
The mime of mesmerisation
On the brink
Between cursing and spell invoking
The stoking of existential rage
The age of collapse and deep adaptation
Of relapse and deep restoration
On the brink
Between falling and rising together
The mime of the river's flow
This is the time of letting go

This is the book of changes
The look of strangers
On the fulcrum
Between inertia and tipping points
The slipping joints of bridges built
The guilt of ignorance and deep knowledge
Of silence and deep homage
On the fulcrum
Between clues and complex ciphers
The look of unlocked mysteries
This is the book of histories

Part 3.

This is the song of shapeshifting
The throng of masks lifting
On the lip
Between captive and running wild
The inner child of selfish choices
The voices of instinct and deep hunger
Of eyes blinked and deep wonder
On the lip
Between hunting and invisible trails
The throng of shadows under the moon
This is the song without a tune

This is the moment of metamorphosis
The atonement for a life of bliss
On the edge
Between sleep and fresh awakening
The breaking in of unworn shoes
The blues of change and deep dreaming
Of sinister and deep scheming
On the edge
Between destruction and recreation
The atonement shedding of old skin
This is the moment for new life to begin

This is the time of transition
The crime of indecision
On the rim
Between breakdowns and breakthroughs
The fake news of puppets in power
The hour of crisis and deep meaning
Of thrown dices and deep greening
On the rim
Between extinction and regeneration
The prime of life's vital virility
This is the time of possibility.

Stepping Up

If all you read are headlines, when the
      nights are long

And your days are crammed with deadlines,
      sometimes

The world can seem a gloomy place, a tired
      space

Of fighting and blighting and struggling to
      make ends meet,

Of snatching victory from the jaws of defeat,
      and yet

In the midst of crises that show no signs of
      letting up

I see you stepping up, I see you getting up

And taking control of your life, I see you
      setting up

The conditions for success, patiently
      building a dream,

Knowing that each brick and beam is an
      investment,

A testament to hard work and foresight, to
      the light

Beyond the storm, to the calm beyond the
      chaos,

For there have always been hard times, and
      those

Who step up to the challenge, who manage
to cope

Because their hope lies not in wishes but in
action,

Who find traction in solutions, rather than
being stuck

In the mire of problems and the wire of
snares, who,

Like you, are stepping up and striding out
and shining bright.

Fifty-Three

The taper of time glimmers and burns

Flaring and fluttering

Spitting and sputtering

While the spectre of space shimmers and
churns

Foaming and fomenting

Reeling and relenting

And at the gnarly nexus of time and space

I must seize my moment and take my place

My light may shine bright, or dim as a glow

My path may lead straight, or bend like a
bow

Still I'll pass on the flame, keep on planting
a tree

I'll be part of the change – crack the code
fifty-three

The days of the year have trickled and
surged

Etching and eroding

Fulfilled and foreboding

While the ways of the past are kindled and
purged

Melting and misfiring

Inking and inspiring

And at the fateful fulcrum of future and
past

I must battle with ghosts and fight for what
lasts

My sword may be blunt, or sharp as my
fear

My feet may be slow, or swift as a deer

Still I'll give it my best, with those stood
beside me

I'll step into the breach – bear the flag fifty-
three

The trails of the sun have burnished and
    honed

Luring and languishing

Vexing and vanquishing

While the voices of doubt have whispered
    and moaned

Chastening and chattering

Niggling and nattering

Still the taper keeps burning, my days
    trickle by

The spectre keeps churning, new ways
    kindle fire

The nexus keeps seeding, my fulcrum is
    poised

The sun-trails are leading, new voices bring
    joys

I'll give thanks for the love, and be all I can
    be

There's a road-trip ahead – up on route
    fifty-three.

This is the Way

No matter what you do or say
Your life is yours to live each day
No matter how you work or play
Your time is yours to spend each day

Take care of where you live and how
Take care of where you work and why
Take care of who you love and how
Take care of who you are and why

No matter if you go or stay
Your life is lived within the fray
No matter if your skies turn grey
Your love is bright – This Is The Way.

The Earth Turns

The Earth turns
Each year brings change
The sea churns
Each wave seeds rains
The mind learns
Each thought plays games
The heart yearns
Each beat sparks flames

A love that's lost can reappear
A hidden face can be revealed
A soul that's hurt can turn from fear
A sacred scroll can be unsealed

The world spins
Each day brings light
The path twists
Each boon or blight
The stream flows
Each ripple bright
The dawn sings
Each wish takes flight.

Moon Whisper

Each year, I scratch and fumble to make
     my mark

Set ink to page, a searchlight in the dark

Not knowing how the letters land, hit or
     miss

Yet they remind us both to follow our bliss

Each year, I muse and mumble to say my
     bit

Patch heart to sleeve, bat wings that glide
     and flit

Not knowing if the moon whispers above
     you

Nor if, like me, it murmurs: I love you.

Rise in the Darkness

I rise in the darkness
So that I may know the beauty of dawn
And appreciate the joy of daylight

And when, in the night, I cannot sleep
I listen to the soothing wisdom of poets
And conjure the spells of magicians

I wander in cold solitude
So that I may feel the glow of home's hearth
And celebrate the warmth of friends

And when, in the wilderness, I am lost
I sing the ancient songs of the land
And dance to the rhythm of nature

I move in the sunshine
So that I may be in sync with time's passing
And forget the vast stillness of space

And when, in the day, I cannot wake
I rally to the cry of revolutionaries
And shake myself from the coma of routine

I tremble with fevered passion
So that I might long for calm quietude
And value the emptiness of mind

And when, in spring, I cannot rest
I gather the secrets of flowers
And dream the whispered sighs of autumn

I rise in the darkness
So that I may know the kiss of waking
And appreciate the gift of being alive.

Fifty-Two

The year began in buoyant mood
A welcome changing of the guard
But dark clouds soon began to brood
And when it came, the rain fell hard

With COVID's armies in retreat
New battle lines were being drawn
With every victory comes defeat
The deepest calm's before the storm

The fallen king clung to his throne
His rabble swarmed the hallowed hill
A desperate dog without his bone
Defiant of the people's will

Then came the bitter toll of war
As lives and livelihoods were lost
The greed of wanting ever more
We count the countless human cost

The spring still spread its carpet bloom
Then summer struck with scorching heat
The autumn leaves fell much too soon
Then winter lay her frozen sheet

We must act now, it's not too late
We must do more than just survive
To help the world regenerate
To help all life to grow and thrive

Despite it all, life carries on
I'm grateful that we made it through
Each day of love's a victory won
I fall and rise at fifty-two.

Not What You See

I am not what you see
Whether ugly or beautiful
Fabulous or forgettable
In your eyes

This visage is a mirage
A mishmash of random genes
A splish-splash of changing scenes
A laughable disguise

I am not what I seem
Whether strong or pathetic
Uninteresting or magnetic
In your unseeing

This mystery is a history
A storm-form of wild schemes
A whirl-swirl of bright dreams
A brilliant being.

I Miss You

It's not that I am lost or lonely
Or have no ways to fill my days
It's just that I would like to kiss you
That is to say, I miss you

It's not that I am tired or tearful
Or have no sky in which to fly
It's just that I recall the bliss you
Bring to my nights, I miss you

It's not that I am dazed or dreamy
Or have no star to reach afar
It's just that I'm in love and wish you
Here with me, I miss you.

Against the Odds

We met upon the battlefield
And you, a warrior for the cause
Defending all the rights of those
Who journeyed to our distant shores

We found our love in forests green
And there, your wounds began to heal
The wooden staff I carved by hand
Replaced the weary sword of steel

We set off on an unknown trail
That rose to meet a mountain range
The sun reflected in your eyes
Inspired us both to make a change

We each discovered hidden paths
New ways in which to learn and lead
And now a movement lives and breathes
Because we planted that first seed

We found our bliss beneath the trees
Our cottage made into a home
It is our refuge from the storm
No matter where we reach and roam

We met against the odds of fate
Now those you love are by your side
I'm lucky to be one of them
To hold your hand with joy and pride.

Sculpted Life, Crafted Love

Each life is like a block of stone
With endless possibility
And as we live, we hew and hone
Our dreams of who we want to be
Each choice we make, each chance
    unknown
Unveils a face of mystery
Each flag we plant, each throw of bones
Brings clarity to what we see

Each love is like a quilt being sewn
With stories of eternity
And as we love, we're not alone
Like roots entangled tree-to-tree
Each risk we take, each layer shown
Reveals another hidden key
Each season brings us nearer home
Upon the journey to be free.

Fifty-One

There are years that crawl and years that
    fly
Years that succeed where others can but
    try
Some years are bursting at the seams
While others scarcely have the means

I've known the years that stick, or change
The years at home and years that range
Sometimes the years are bold and bright
While other years stay black as night

With fifty-one years laid to rest
The last was walked in valleys low
A year that put me to the test
A shadow out of which to grow.

New Day

Sunset bleeds in crimson sky

Black night brings respite, rest and
    reflection

Purple dawn promises new day.

All In

We took a risk and rolled the dice
We took the salty with the spice
There was a chance we'd lose or win
We took our chips and went all in

The cards we held were dealt by chance
We played without a second glance
Only to find, amidst the haze
We found a pathway through the maze

Was it just luck or something more
That led us to each other's door?
Against the odds, or destiny?
I bet on you, you bet on me

We chose for hope and spun the wheel
We chose the wishes to make real
There was a chance we'd sink or swim
We took our love an went all in.

In the Margins

When the story of my life is writ
All the chapters set, the headings bold
You may miss the most important bit
For it's in the margins life is told

You may spot the notes in spidery hand
Crammed alongside work and daily grind
All the treasures of events unplanned
And creative doodles of the mind

They may not connect to life's main plot
Or the tidy order on display
They may be the things that time forgot
Or the flash of colour in the grey

The main narrative may well be true
But it misses chaos, love and flair
It may chart the course on which I flew
Yet say nothing of my soul's great dare

All the times I detoured and got lost
Or indulged in poetry and art
When I gave and did not count the cost
Or glimpsed the whole beyond the parts

When the story of my life is told
When the scribbling pen has come to rest
Just remember, as the tale unfolds
It's in the margins that I lived the best.

A Poem

A poem's the sound we hear when words go
out to play

As they romp and rhyme, laugh and cry, or
go astray

Some play nice, while others scratch and
swear in fights

Some get down and dirty, some climb to
heady heights

A poem's the show we see when words are
on display

As they flit and flirt bright colours, or
shades of grey

Some paint true, while others splash and
scatter with shapes

Some tell epic stories, some clown around
with japes

A poem's the churn we feel when words are
in the fray

As they lilt and love, muse and mourn, or
quietly pray

Some are thieves, while others shine and
selflessly give

Some spark the fire of hope, some teach us
how to live.

Fifty

In all my years upon the Earth
This was the strangest since my birth
The year the ghostly virus struck
When time stood still and things got stuck

A year locked down under the dome
A chance to think, to be at home
A year of sickness and of death
When nature took a gasping breath

The crystal streams, the silent sky
The empty streets, the question why
The heartbeat of a world at rest
A seismic pause, a global test

Although we mourn for what is lost
We must reflect and count the cost
Of what will be our child's regret
If we ignore the Great Reset

The end of coal, the peak of oil
The time to restore living soil
The promise of a solar dawn
An end to night, a brand-new dawn

A year of distance and of fear
A chance to love all we hold dear
A year of endings and of pain
When all good things must start again

Whatever challenges we face
This is our moment to embrace
A bigger view, a longer range
My fiftieth, the Year of Strange.

African Flame

You are the first spark that kindles the fire
That nurtures our daring and restless
    desire
On journeys across the wilderness plain
You light up the way: our African flame

You are the red bloom that graces the tree
That rises from ash, a wonder to see
In nature resplendent, we honour your
    name
You burn with great beauty: our African
    flame

You are the fierce blaze that forges the soul
That touches the sky and makes the earth
    whole
Through hardship and toil, in fortune and
    fame
You burn with great faith: our African flame

You are the hot coal that glows in the night

That gives us the strength to stand up and
fight

Deep passion's a fire nobody can tame

You burn with great hope: our African
flame

You are the warm light that keeps off the
cold

That cradles our dreams and stories of old

Together in strength, diverse and the same

You burn with great love: our African flame

You are the enigma that flickers with heat

That dances with drums in sync to the beat

With colours that shine, with stars in your
aim

You brighten the world: our African flame.

All the Colours

The very moment that we met
I knew we would be best of friends
It started back in Tott'nham days
But that's not how the story ends

As both our lives began to change
New partners and new purpose too
We seemed to move in swaying sync
With worlds unfolding bright and new

Now when I think of you, I smile
Recalling cider wisdom shared
And all the colours of your life
A sign of one who dreamed and dared

Today your sun's on painted sky
With fresh adventures to begin
A flower shows your essence true
Of beauty blooming from within.

This is the Place

This is the place we dreamed of
And we dreamed it into being
This is the home we talked of
And our words have turned to seeing

Each day, we see the pine and oaks
And hear the birds a-singing
Each day, we see the garden grow
And send our hopes a-winging

This is the place we've landed
And we're sure to put down roots
This is the home we've chosen
And now we'll put out shoots

Each day, we test our limits
And reach out for the light
Each day, we spread our knowledge
And shine our colours bright

This is the place we wished for
And our wishes have come true
This is the home we share now
And our lives begin anew.

The Things We've Been Through

Looking back, I'm amazed
At the things we've been through
At each step, how we've blazed
A new trail made for two

How we've travelled up mountains
To temples and streams
Across beaches, to fountains
Through forests of dreams

All the things we've been through
In all kinds of foul weather
When the pandemic grew:
Isolation together!

How we've worked on the move
Found a beautiful home
How we've danced to the groove
Of the places we roam

When we fell or we flew
Nearly drowning at sea
All the things we've been through
Showed us what we can be

As we've wended our ways
How our love has stayed true
Looking back through the maze
At the things we've been through.

Spirited Away

One fine day, I'll let myself be
Spirited away, to a world yet unseen
In the grey, the mist of a dream
Where sprites play and nature nymphs
    stream
Amidst the spray of waterfalls and green
Forests, a ray of sunshine, a beam
Of light, a stray path in between.

One day soon, I'll let myself go
To the moon, to the stars that glow
Like the bloom of ideas, the flow
Of a tune of memories that grow
And then swoon, like the winds blow
Across the dune and the swirling snow
Paints a plume on skies I used to know

One dark night, I'll let myself fly
Out of sight, out of mind, with a sigh
I'll take flight, let loose every tie
Every plight that weighs and asks why
Every fight won or lost, on a high
Of pure light, I'll laugh and I'll cry
With delight, I'll be spirited away by and by.

Forty-Nine

Another drop in life's great sea
Another drop that ripples free
Into the ocean, vast yet changed
With tidal currents rearranged
For every drop's a vital clue
To secrets hidden in the blue
Another drop for forty-nine
Another drop into the brine
Where secrets in the swirl of days
Are whispered drops of crystal ways
While tidal breaths still rise and fall
The ocean moves the life of all
Another drop of destiny
Another drop: that drop is me.

Fleeting

I'm writing these words
Without too much to say
Except that I'm thinking
Of you on this day

Our words are so fleeting
Like birds in the sky
They often say what
And seldom say why

I'm writing these symbols
Without riddle or code
Except that life's cipher
Unlocks love on the road

Our letters are bottles
That float on the sea
They reach distant shores
And set their words free

I'm writing this letter
Without reason or rhyme
Except that our bonding
Transcends space and time.

Home

Home is the centre of love
That we create with and for each other
Home is the safe space
Where we can be ourselves, unmasked
Home is the place of joy
Brought alive by family and friends

When we are weary
Home is the resting place of rejuvenation
When we are winning
Home is the swirling room of victory
    dancing
When we are dreaming
Home is the flaming hearth of endless
    possibility

Home is setting down roots
For a day, a year or a lifetime
Home is our treasure chest
To store shared memories, old and new
Home is our small piece of earth
To take care of and nurture together.

Forty-Eight

That time of year has come again
To mark the page with ink and pen
To mark the turn of mortal wheel
To down the lights and play the reel

The story flickers, scene to scene
My path of life upon the screen
Some faces shine while others fade
Some chase the sun, some hide in shade

There's love and action in the plot
Some lines recalled and some forgot
There's drama too, some glitz and gloss
Starbursts of joy and caves of loss

Some parts seem tailor-made to bore
Routines repeated as before
But then there's magic breaking through
From dust of old, the glint of new

The tale meanders, unforeseen
From bushveld beige to desert green
Through cities grey to bays of blue
Each place a world of shifting hue

I cannot read the runes of dreams
This march of days, this swirl of means
I simply throw the bones of fate
And close the loop at forty-eight.

Crook O'Lune

A cabin nestled by the trees
A trickling stream, a rustling breeze
A cosy home, a drifting tune
Our sanctuary, our Crook O'Lune

A river flowing through the dale
An arching bridge, a snaking trail
A cloudy sky, a peeping moon
Our place of peace, our Crook O'Lune

A woodland in the hills of green
A change of pace, a tranquil scene
A fair display of nature's boon
Our calm retreat, our Crook O'Lune

A couple on the path of love
A field below, vast skies above
A season turns, unveils a rune
Our mystery, our Crook O'Lune.

Graduation

You've mastered your mind
One summit's behind
More peaks like ahead
More dreams to be fed
Now lead from the heart
You've just made a start
And we'll be by your side
Always bursting with pride.

Life Goes On

Life goes on

But do not say that nothing has changed

For a beautiful light has gone from this
world

Leaving a black spot on the sun of my days

Life goes on

But do not act like nothing is out of place

For a silver strand has been cut from life's
web

Leaving a loose thread in the weave of my
love

Life goes on

But do not think that nothing is lost

For an incredible story has come to an end

Leaving an empty space in the stars of my
sky

Life goes on

And so will I, given time and given space

For the light and the love and the story live
on

Leaving a luminous trail to guide my ways.

Memory Stones

The cold is biting, the darkness
     disorientating
in the hollow caves of loss, the waves
of anger, the shades of sadness, the
     madness
of life when it rips from the roots, when it
shoots poison arrows and leaves us
     bleeding
and battered, pleading and shattered, yet
alive, breathing and seething, while breath
was stolen from others, without warning,
without reason, they are dead

The sun still rises, the earth turns, as if
nothing changed; it's strange, as if
no one noticed the flames, the screaming,
the crashing down of a life, the smashing
to pieces of plans and dreams and what
     might
have been; the cold, grey ashes of a love
that burned bright and brief, too brief,
now grief is all that's left, the theft is
complete, the mortal coil is shed

The stones remain, memories from the
        burning
hearth, the bright blaze of living, the giving
of shape and form to who they were and
        what
they did, to what we did together, forever
cherished, pebbles in my mind, treasures
yet to find, a weight of shared times and
special places, remembered faces, traces of
adventures and folly, a patterned mosaic,
celebration of a life, enough said.

Forty-Seven

A year of sailing restless seas
In search of waters calm
Until we found a friendly port
To shelter us from harm
We dropped an anchor of content
A respite from the swell
To nurture gritty dream into
A pearl inside the shell

Now as we wake, cathedral bells
Ring out a welcome song
Down cobbled streets, in lecture halls
We glow while nights grow long
Our next adventure's just begun
Beneath a spangled heaven
Upon the cusp of earth and tide
In harbour forty-seven.

Mountain View

A barren place of grass and clay
A vision planted true
From tender care and patient work
Emerged our Mountain View

A paradise of birds and trees
Beneath the skies of blue
With brown thatched roofs and welcome
    guests
Now stands our Mountain View

A place to rest, a place to heal
To see the world anew
We journey on, yet in our hearts
Springs green our Mountain View.

Lost Key

I. The Key

It was just a glimpse
A glint in the sun
A flint spark in the park
As I walked along
Lost in a daze
Amidst the maze of thoughts
And paths not taken
Futures forsaken
A flash of something
Out of place in space
And time
A rhyme interrupted
On its steady march
I glanced askance
To find the source
Of my distraction
That point of light
Which changed the course
Of flight in action

And there it lay, an object astray
Dull upon the vivid grass
Like glass that's lost
Its sheen and shine
Until the rays
Of blue-lit days break through
The haze of dappled tree:
It was a key

II. The Lock

I bent and picked
Then gently flicked
The metal trinket free of dust
Thumbed its dent
And stroked its rust
My eyes mesmerised
By its jagged edge
And ragged mystery
Its silent history
Of openings
Of protecting and concealing
Hidden treasures
The pleasures of unlocking and revealing
An unknown nest
Of artefacts
A chest of gold
Or letters old
And fading, the lines shading
In the trace of stories
Of star struck lovers
Or soldiers' glories and grieving mothers

Or something more mundane
A plain account of transactions
Between two parties
Now estranged, the tick and tock
Of a broken clock:
Behind the lock

III. The Keyholder

I began to meditate
Upon the lost key's heft and shape
An object cleft from fire and steel
To reveal something
So unique, like fingerprints
Like hints of who
And clues to why
The echoed cry of one
The puzzle
Of how this story's begun
I find myself wondering
Pacing and pondering
Tracing the mists of the owner's travels
The twists and turns
The burns and blisters
As fate's tapestry unravels
Leaving these fragments
Like loose threads
Fraying through life's seasons
The reasons long since lost
The untold cost of living

Of giving without getting
Of letting
The most precious things
Disappear on wings of regret
For we forget, as we get older:
We're the keyholder

IV. The Box

Keys without locks are castaways
Unhanded and stranded
On faraway shores
Where the cause of their being
The eye of their seeing is blinded
So as I held in my palm
This enigma, this charm
I could tell that its spell
Was unbroken
I had stumbled and fumbled upon a token
With a secret unspoken
And now in my power, this synchronous
            hour
I could grant a dying wish
A moment of bliss
It's crazy I know
Yet I felt a deep flow
A tide in my head, blood red
Tugging and teasing
Ice logic unfreezing
Like a serpent in search of its tail

In a flash it came through
The thing I must do
For I knew without fail
That this was the key
That the future unlocks
And the fit was with me:
I was the box.

Forty-Six

I nearly drowned, this year gone by
A feeble, frightful way to die
The waves too rough, the tide too strong
A frolic in the surf gone wrong

The year itself was full and bright
(There is no shadow without light):
My lovely daughter turned eighteen
My nephew earned the keys to life
My work took flight on silver screen
The year was peaceful, without strife

We nearly drowned, my love and I
Beneath that sunny summer sky
Dragged out to sea, the undertow
We feared it was our time to go

The other days were amply spent
On journeys, near and far, we went:
From pyramids and jungles green
To mirrored lakes and canyon walls
From mountains, caves and crystal streams
To crescent sands and gothic halls

We nearly drowned, first of July
With no regrets and no goodbye
The ocean made its power known
(At least we'd not have died alone)

The life we live is ebb and flow
The winters come, the summers go:
At times, the world is fresh and new
Love buds and blooms and casts its spell
At times, we barely make it through
We ache, we breathe, we live to tell

I nearly drowned, this year gone by
There are no rhymes or reasons why
But I'm still here, still in the mix
Alive and well at forty-six.

What Now? (The Unpopular Vote)

What now?
He won the unpopular vote
What now?
He's an emperor without any coat
What now?
All the power's in the hands of a fool
What now?
We're all living under bigotry's rule

Now we rise up and we speak out
For this is the hour of democracy's test
Now we defend the freedoms he flouts
For this is the moment to fight for our best
Now we dig deep and we stand tall
For this is the day for our values to shine
Now we defend and we don't fall
For this is the moment for holding the line

For our freedom and justice
We'll march on the street
For our planet and climate
We'll turn up the heat
For our women and children
We'll make our voice heard
For the sake of our future
We'll not be deterred

Now we take stock and we prepare
For this is the hour of our reckoning
Now we join up and we share
For this is the moment of beckoning
Now we align and we support
For this is the day of pulling together
Now we get tough and we retort
For this is the moment to brave out the
        weather

For the keepers of every faith
We'll refuse to be divided
For the people of every race
We'll refuse to be one-sided
For the young ones and the old
We'll find a better direction
For the willing and the bold
We'll fight until the next election

What now?
We take up the strain on the rope
What now?
We stand with the forces of hope
What now?
We declare for the rights we have won
What now?
We unite and take action as one.

Magic Feather

I'm giving you this feather
To remind you of the endless sky
That even when you feel earthbound
You still have glorious wings to fly

I know life's not all sunshine
And you won't escape the aching pain
But like water off a mallard's back
You too can shrug off driving rain

There's power in this feather
To remind you of your magic flights
That even when you crash your landings
You still can rise to brilliant heights

I know love's not all roses
And not all tales have a happy end
But like water from the sacred springs
You too can purify and mend

So hold onto this feather
To remind you that your future's bright
That even when your feet are muddy
Your spirit's always light.

Goddess of the Sum

There are gods for the planets
And gods for the turbulent seas
But the Mother of Daylight
Is the goddess for mortal me

You're the blush on my skin
The glint in my evergreen eyes
You're the dream I begin
The blaze in my overcast skies

There are nymphs of the rivers
And sylphs of the pellucid air
But the Lady of Lumen
Is a deva more filigree fair

You're the dawn of my light
The phosphorescence of my Milky Way
You're the torch in my night
The incandescence of my golden ray

There is Sól and Apollo
Helios, Anyanwu and Ra
But all of them must kowtow
To a deity much brighter by far

You're the cartwheel in my galaxy
The twinkle in my rising star
You're the fire in my firmament
The one I love, my Indi-Ra.

Futuristic Man

A futuristic man I am
I am a future's man
I come to you across the blue
I come to you I do

I am a hop ahead of you
Just like a kangaroo
And if you listen on the wind
You'll hear my didgeridoo

If I'm down under, what are you?
You must be over up
So if you stand upon your head
We'll be the same, with luck

When you're awake, I am asleep
And when you sleep I wake
No chance to meet in life or dreams
To trick the clock of fate

A futuristic man I am
I am a future's man
I come to you across the blue
It's true, I come to you.

Haiku 4

Curtains slowly part
Beauty is revealed as art
Now the play can start.

Haiku 5

A sting in the tail
Is neither poison nor pain
But a fire's glow.

We Never Kissed

We sipped wine to a starling serenade
And dropped clues in our muted
    masquerade
We best-dressed in veils of cotton and silk
And fine-dined on tales of popcorn and milk

We spoke in riddles, but captured the gist
We tasted sweet salt, but we never kissed

We marked time to a flickering white flame
And shared space in a lingering love game
We forlorned the loss of an artist king
And flirt-skirted around a fiery ring

We spoke in whispers, but welcomed the
    mist
We tied a frayed knot, but we never kissed.

A Hundred Questions

A hundred questions in the room
And on display, the chosen few:
How can we turn the deadly tide?
And will we spurn our toxic pride?
But in my head, the only clue:
I wonder, did she feel it too?

A hundred questions for our time
Some speak in sculpture, some in rhyme:
How can we change our fate most dire?
And can an artist still inspire?
But more intriguing and sublime:
How does she make her canvass shine?

A hundred questions from the floor
Like scattered gold upon the shore:
How fierce the urgency of now?
And can we turn our swords to plough?
But all that I could plot and draw:
Could we have met somewhere before?

A hundred questions in the air
Some speak of hope, some of despair:
What if our waking is too late?
And what's the dream we can create?
Some questions I could never share:
But did she glimpse enough to care?

A hundred questions from the fray
Like puzzling games for us to play:
        How poetry and science can meet?
And will our planet overheat?
Yet colouring my maze of grey:
I hope we meet again some day?

That Scary Hairy Man

Mommy, don't make me
Please, please don't take me
To see Santa Clause at the mall
There's still time turn back
If I sit on his lap
There's always the chance that I'll fall!

His knees are (ouch!) knobbly
His legs are (yikes!) wobbly
And he has that strange look in his eye
His breath smells (eeew!) funny
His nose is (yuck!) runny
And he says he's got pets that can fly!

So mommy, don't make me
Please mom don't you take me
To see Santa Clause at the mall

His fur hat you'll note
Like his ketchup-red coat
Match the colour of his ruddy nose
And he wiggles his belly
It jiggles like jelly
Every time he erupts with ho-hos!

There's still time turn back
'Cos my favourite cap
Is at home, mom, I've just now recalled

His sack's full of toys
For good girls and boys
But you said 'don't take presents from
strangers'
He's got fairies and elves
And wild reindeers by twelves
Really mom, there's no end to the dangers!

So please please don't make me
Mommy, don't take me
To see Santa Clause at the mall

But if you insist
I'll tell him my list
I'll be brave, mom, I'll give it a try
But he's all big and hairy
Quite frankly, he's scary
So don't be surprised if I cry!

It's too late to turn back
I just sat on his lap
And he whispered I had a great haul
Of gifts there for me
Waiting under the tree
Thanks mom, I like Santa after all!

Look After Your Heart

I hear your warning:

Look after your heart, you've been hurt
    before

When strangers approach, don't open the
    door

Take care who you trust, don't risk love too
    soon

Don't sway with the tide, don't swing with
    the moon

Yet I am thinking:

A bird in a cage is safe but not free

A plant in a pot won't grow to a tree

A wood is not light unless there's a path

A home is not warm unless there's a hearth

So I have resolved:

To open my heart, not hide anymore

To welcome new friends, like waves to the
    shore

To give trust a chance, give into love's
    swoon

Let hope hum its song, and dance to the
    tune.

Africa Calls To Me

Africa calls to me
And I hear her voice
In the beat of drums that echo the rhythm
  of my days
And the lilt of songs that rock the lullaby of
  my nights
In the twist of tales that guide the journey
  of my ways
And the sigh of breath that swirls the dance
  of my flights

Africa speaks to me
And I listen to her words
In the surging roar of the lion that awakens
  my belief
And the silly laugh of the hyena that helps
  me to cope
In the soft rumble of the elephant that fills
  me with relief
And the gentle stir of the gorilla that revives
  my hope

The sounds of Africa

Are the cries of the world's first born and
      forgotten child

Taking us back into the womb of creation

The sounds of Africa

Are the songs of the world's sacred and
      untamed wild

Placing our hearts on the altar of oblation

When I am close by

Africa's sounds reach into me

With the crackle of village campfires that
      light my skies

And the rattle of machine gunfire that
      shatters my calm

With the rustle of timid wildlife that
      answers my sighs

And the bustle of busy town life that sings
      my psalm

Africa calls to me

And I hear her drum

In the canyon cry of the fish eagle that frees
my soul

And the desert hush of the sand dune that
soothes my mind

In the forest call of the loerie that makes me
whole

And the bushveld drone of the cicada that
blots out time

When I am far away

Africa's voice cries out to me

With the crashing of ocean waves that hug
her shores

And the lashing of phantom slaves that
haunt her past

With the rumbling of thunder clouds that
drench her pores

And the crumbling of plunder plots that
cannot last

The sounds of Africa
Are the screams of the world's deepest and
        darkest fears
Yearning for the light of emancipation
The sounds of Africa
Are the words of the world's most wise and
        neglected seers
Pointing towards the star of salvation

Africa sings to me
And I listen to her song
In the babbling of bright markets that
        buffet my senses
And the lament of lone hawkers that
        pervade my dreams
In the buzz of packed stadiums that lower
        my defences
And the hoot of crammed taxis that mimic
        my screams

Africa calls to me

And I answer her call

Though my whisper is drowned in the
cacophony of despair

And my tune wanders in the maze of
melodies lost and found

Yet I remain captivated by the symphony
we share:

A perfect score of light and a pure
celebration of sound.

Exquisite Pain

Fresh wounds of first light trickle blood-red
at dawn

The past has been shattered, the present is
torn

Broad swathes of bruised clouds blanket
over the sky

A storm charged with longing and aches of
goodbye

Cold hands of grey fog settle over the earth

The chill of love's shadow, the womb of
rebirth

Dark nights of the soul bring on lashings of
rain

All these are life's moments of exquisite
pain.

Faith: In Memoriam

I never will forget the day
My faith in people passed away -

I loved her true, I thought she cared
Yet innocence could not be spared
For fairytales of simple truth
Are fantasies spun for the youth

She did not stop to count the cost
Of what was gained and what was lost
She took in hand deception's knife
And made the choice to take a life

Her aim was sure, the cut was deep
(No mercy when the past is cheap)
No armour worn, my heart-wound bled
Until my trusting self was dead

It does not help to mourn or cry
Some things can live and some must die
For naïve hope there is no place
And love can leave without a trace -

But I never will forget the day
My faith in people passed away.

Iambic Pentameter

The marching rhythm of a pair of feet
Stride boldly out across the empty page
The subtle stepping of a word-trod beat
Gives cadence echoed throughout every age
The pulse of poets history repeats.

The Vision of You

The vision of you -
Dances in my white rain
Shines in my violet sky
Flashes in my indigo storm
Ripples in my blue lake
Shimmers in my green forest
Drifts in my yellow sand
Meanders in my orange canyon
Melts in my red sunset
Twinkles in my black night -
You of the vision.

A Moment's Silence Please

A moment's silence please
For the new life not conceived
For the first breath not breathed

A moment's silence please
For the little baby never born
For the tiny outfits never worn.

Possession

Why this mad possession
This jealous obsession
With phantom demons
In search of reasons?

Why this compulsive desire
This unquenchable fire
To hurt and maim
Regardless of blame?

Paralysed

We recruit for the long run, they said
Only the best
A cut above the rest
Those who will stand the test
Of pressure and time
And the bottom line
But they lied
I was cast aside
At the first turn of the tide
Now I'm left paralysed

It made no difference
That I committed body and soul
Met every goal
More than fulfilled my role
They sucked me dry
Then someone cast the die
The memo was sent
And my life was rent
Apart
At the heart

My number was called

Something about the organisation being
overhauled

Downsized

Rightsized

(Right for who?)

So they lied

And I am left

Bereft

Paralysed

People are our most important asset, they
said

Yet how quick they are to trash it

As soon as they can cash it

And do not tell me the process is fair

When it depends on the square

You land on

The label they brand on

Ladders for up, snakes for down

There's only one game in town

And it's built on lies

Someone always dies

Or, like me, is left paralysed

There are other opportunities, they said
But my heart's no longer in it
They can take it and bin it
I refuse to hobnob
To get a new job
When I've only just been robbed
Something has died inside
Maybe it's pride
But I'm getting wise
To their lies
That have left me paralysed

I guess I'll have to snap out of it, I say
But I don't really know how
For now
I can't see what is to gain
By going through the pain
All over again
I'm just coping
Hoping
That along the way
The sun will shine on a new day
That I'll see the world through new eyes

That my life will re-energise
And rise
Above the lies
I so despise
That keep me paralysed.

Innocent Words

Innocent words
Drip like poison
Seeping into my bones
Twisting my reason
Churning my emotions
Gripping my heart
Innocent words

Invisible words
Make her smile
Make her laugh
Make her happy
Keep her engaged
They are not my words
Invisible words

Friendly words
Tick tick tick
On the keyboard
On the clock
An evening of togetherness
Slowly evaporates
Friendly words

Angry words
Fill my head
They are not for her
They are for me
Me, me, selfish me
They must not escape
Angry words

Manic words
What madness is this?
That makes me hurt
The one I love
Push away
The one I want to hold close
Manic words

Silent words
Soothe self-inflicted wounds
The language of touch
Speaks what I cannot say
Whispers I love you
Prays forgive me
Silent words.

Power-Suit

There was a time when I ruled the universe
In my batman mask and superman cape
Changing the fate of nations and planets
Limited only by the power of imagination

Now it is I who am ruled by the world
In my manager mask and tailor-made suit
Changing nothing that amounts to much
Limited only by the power of conformity

I remember a time when I ran barefoot free
In my scruffy shorts and worn-out shirt
Eager to play and curious to discover
Living for the moment and judging by the
        heart

Now I walk the narrow corridors of power
In my leather shoes and silken tie
Eager to win and driven to dominate
Living for the future and judging by the
        past

And yet, inside, I am no different than
    before

I am still that boy, running wild and living
    free

Ever-ready for fun and poised to change
    destiny

There's more to this power-suit than meets
    the eye!

Tinkerbelle

Oh magic muse, from whence art thou?
Streaking bright across my midnight sky
With twinkle toes
And sparkling eyes
Cheeky pose
And tempting smile
A trail of light, between then and now
Sprinkling pixie-dust, that I might fly.

Harmony

Sunset beach
Silhouette
Couple hand in hand
Pebble wish
Crashing waves
Footprints in the sand

Dim-lit room
Jasmine scent
Rhythm of a drum
Tidal dance
Currents swirl
Bodies move as one.

Voyeurs of Terror

The first news strikes like lightening -

Blasting the tranquil skies of a humdrum
day

Blinding the startled vision of an
unbelieving world

Blanching the numbed mind of a fragile
civil sanity

The reports start to trickle in, icy cold -

Aeroplane Collides with Trade Centre in
New York City

Second Tower Hit in Suspected Terror
Attack

Pentagon in Flames as Third Suicide
Mission Strikes

The dam of information breaks,
overwhelming -

Towers Collapse, Thousands Killed, Chaos
Erupts

Fourth Plane Down Over Uninhabited Area

America, The World, Switches to Red Alert!

Waves of aftershock follow the earthquake
events -

Geopolitical elders face a new landscape of
canyons and bridges

Religious tribes find no refuge in caves of
peace and love

Economic prophets shudder as runaway
cracks appear in money and markets

We watch with guilty anticipation

As the world declares war

On its shadow.

Scientist, Artist, Businessman

I imagine being a scientist –
Striving to understand what appears to be
 …
I dream of being an artist –
Yearning to express what might be …
And yet, I am a businessman –
Exploiting and manipulating what is.

Your Spirit is Light

Like a paratrooper
You took the leap
Into the great beyond
Like a frog
Forsaking the safety of the land
For the shimmering pond
Now you tarry awhile
With the next lily pad
Almost in sight
Remembering that in life
It is your buoyancy of spirit
That makes you light.

Remember the Forest

May the year ahead
Contain the variety of the seasons
The growth of the trees
The connection to all life
May you suffer out the wind
Stand firm in the storms
Turn your leaves to the sun
And remember the Forest.

The Circle is Drawn

Bob Steyn: In Memoriam

like a burst of light
you came into my dark night of confusion
like a cool fount of crystal water
in a desert of dogma left behind

as you named and blessed my kin
the wisdom of your words anointed me too
the veil was rent
the scattered puzzle begun anew
the old shapes of the cross outgrown
in your wider circle I found a new home

as I left your sacred chapel
I knew I would return
for this was a place of love
and searching
where my flaming quest could burn

in time, you became my teacher-friend
receiving my letters

meeting to talk at noontime
like a bowl catching the spilt water
of my ideas and conflicts
only to nourish the budding multi-coloured
     flowers
of my consciousness

but the grabbing hands outstretched
for your healing words and touch
with office pressures and ministerial duties
became too much
our scheduled space ended
it was time for me to fly alone
carried by the expansive wings
of the philosophy we now shared

my navigator's map
(a gift from you)
set a course
for we Aquarian Conspirators
a new breathing together
a shifting paradigma
now I knew
I was not alone

in ritual, counsel and celebration
you walked with me through the valleys
when my name symbolised my quest
my family offended and I misunderstood
when crime shattered my peace
my home my body my mind violated

also you scaled with me the peaks
sometimes guide
always fellow seeker of new vistas
when I was welcomed into the Unitarian
    family
recognised among liberal thinkers
when I celebrated twenty-one years of life
embracing freedom with responsibility
when two hearts became one
filling each other's cups

onward you continued your steadfast
    service
the brilliance of your sun and moon shining
    bright
but like a secret witness
I caught fleeting glimpses

of the flickering shadows of fatigue
which threatened to eclipse the light
yet you shone forth
burdened
yet uplifted
by a needy world
and days so finite

this poem is incomplete
ended too soon
like your life it would seem
but the circle is drawn
like the serpent with tail in mouth
every ending a new beginning
every death
a new life.

Diggers and Dreamers

Diggers and dreamers are we,
Slaving that we might be free;
Meanwhile our Mother Earth bleeds,
To satisfy men's hungry needs
For riches and glory and wealth.

Mecca

Each of us needs to travel
The road to Mecca
Our Mecca –
Our city of light
Where we take on our apprenticeship
And ultimately,
Where we return
As Masters.

Island

Island, sea sand, sunshine, shore
Distant, desolate, alone once more
Not by force, but by own choosing
Undecided - winning, losing?

The Final Test

We're on a path that twists and turns
Through landscapes ever changing
Sometimes it's hard, and so we learn
Through patterns rearranging
The trick, it seems, is not to fight
Against the unexpected
Keep moving on towards the light
And don't become dejected
Easier said than done, I know
Yet that's the final test:
To fall and rise, to love and grow
While letting go the rest.

Perspective

There's a crispy freshness
In all that you do
When your perspective changes
To one that is new.

www.ingramcontent.com/pod-product-compliance
Lightning Source LLC
Chambersburg PA
CBHW051213090426
42742CB00021B/3432